CHINA
City and Exile

A Collection of the Poetry of Place

Edited by
ALEXANDER MONRO

ELAND • LONDON

First published in December 2010 by Eland Publishing Ltd,
61 Exmouth Market, Clerkenwell, London EC1R 4QL

All poems © of the authors and translators, as
attributed in the text and in the acknowledgements

This arrangement and commentary © Alexander Monro

ISBN 978 1 906011 30 7

Pages designed and typeset by Antony Gray
Cover image: Poet on a Mountain Top by
Shen Zhou (1427–1509)
Printed and bound in Spain by GraphyCems, Navarra

Contents

TO JAMIE AND SUSIE

A BRIEF TIMELINE OF RELEVANT CHINESE HISTORY

I spur my horse past ruins;
Ruins move a traveller's heart.
The old parapets high and low
The ancient graves great and small,
The shuddering shadow of a tumbleweed,
The steady sound of giant trees.
But what I lament are the common bones
Unnamed in the records of immortals.

HAN SHAN
translated by Anne Birrell

INTRODUCTION

To become Prime Minister in ancient China, a man had not only to master the classics, but to write good poetry. Even the standard civil service examinations contained a strong element of poetry. No country or kingdom has set so much stock by poetry as China, and few can claim to have produced it in such stunning range and depth, especially given the constraints posed by form in traditional Chinese verse. Several arts have held sway in China's history, among them landscape painting, calligraphy (an integral part of poetry), music and martial disciplines. But poetry has always been considered the highest among them. Among China's classical art forms, it is the most stirring and inviting.

The themes are sometimes different from what you might expect. Death does not feature as prominently as in the western tradition, while widespread suffering often does. Love is of course a focus, especially in the 'decadent' palace poetry of the Song dynasty. The natural world is another regular muse, often accompanied by a Daoist sensibility that fused natural beauty and mystical experience. Li Bai was especially adept at this form. Yet few themes receive more attention in China than loss, from a lady whose husband has run off to war, to a traveller far from home or a courtier banished to the hinterland.

But, of course, the conjuring of life in a city now destroyed, or love in a marriage now divided, allows what is past to appear again, for the poet as for his readership. That is the reason for this collection, a look at the poetry that touches on imperial China's two greatest cities of Chang'an (now Xi'an) and Luoyang. It is an attempt to recreate cities whose character is mostly lost, though can still be uncovered from time to time in a quiet Xi'an lane by night or among the ruined walls of the old city in the fields east of modern Luoyang. These poems recreate either the city itself or the experience of its inhabitants, in order to provide a way back to what it was, and to help the traveller to feel some of the force of its colourful past.

The collection takes poems written over several centuries. While the golden age of Chinese verse was during the Tang (618–907 AD), and the High Tang (around 710–766) in particular, Tang poetry is not exceptionally old within the Chinese tradition. This collection features Tang greats like Li Bai and Du Fu but it also reaches back to the first and second century AD, when Chang'an and Luoyang were already great cities: the Han dynasty. There are a few later poems too, although whereas painting and porcelain reached their heights in the later dynasties, poetry never recovered its Tang vitality or its Song (960–1279) elegance.

But the collection also steps out of the city. Courtiers and scholars alike would leave the city for the mountains to escape the high ritual and shallow sycophancy of the court in the wildness and solitude of the hills beyond. Not all arrived by choice; many were banished, often for a single poem deemed too political.

Picture a man sitting at a desk, brush in hand, looking out towards the mountains, reflecting on his absence from the court and the city. Perhaps he has been banished for criticising the emperor, or perhaps palace eunuchs have conspired to enforce his departure. But now, caught in solitary thought, he is torn between this reclusive life in the ineffability of nature, and the urban glories of the court and of power. This same tension fuelled some of China's greatest verse.

Such a picture could be applied to hundreds of old Chinese poems and it frequently invades my mind as I read them. In it is loss, beauty and dissatisfaction. From it welled poems redolent with the liberty of solitude, yet written by men who could not help but yearn for society once again.

CHANG'AN

Chang'an (now Xi'an) was China's consummate capital, home to the eponymous Han dynasty before they finally moved the capital to Luoyang. A Chang'an legend tells that the supreme emperor first invited the Qin ruler to dinner and bequeathed him the region, and this was why the Qin could become the founders of China. The Qin took power in 211 BC and left an indelible mark, not only in spawning the idea of a unified Chinese kingdom, but also in the solid forms of the terracotta warriors and the vast imperial tomb of Emperor Shi. The tomb still awaits exploration, a process that could last a century.

The city was laid out to face the four points of the compass, while eight surrounding buildings 'were like stars framing the North Star'. According to the Chang'an co-narrator in Ban Gu's fabulous *Poem on the western capital*, its spaces were broad. In the dignitaries' quarter silk tassels and crowns could be seen everywhere 'and carriage canopies were as dense as clouds in the sky'. Just to the south of the city lay the imperial grounds, a thousand *li* of towering hills, and of woods and vales. In the Rear Palaces were 'crowds of modest young women, beautifully adorned – if you saw them you could only admire them'.

Here too were orchards and flowers, springs and canals, an imperial hunting park with horses from Ferghana, rhinoceroses from Huang Zhi, birds from Tao Zhi and unrecognisable species from kingdoms beyond the distant Kunlun mountains, north of the Himalayas. The hunt would take place in the emperor's grounds and afterwards, writes Ban, 'strong men held up weights, acrobats and jugglers performed, choirs sang, dressed as fairies . . . and men in leopard and bear skins danced, while other men dressed as white tigers played on lutes, and green dragons blew their flutes . . . Magicians would suddenly change their appearance and divide their form, swallow swords and breathe out fire'.

In the city itself, the poet relates, order was supreme, with pleasant, raftered houses in rows. Guards protected the nine markets, where fair trade was generally done, although certain traders were prone to 'deceiving dim-witted country folk, and making fools of small-town folk'. The great families used bells to announce meals and ate from large cauldrons. In the hoary city lanes, 'wandering braves' picked fights with one another. Bohemia was never far away either. The city had an imperial music academy and, in the north, a more bohemian quarter for courtesans.

The Han dynasty saw a Chinese mentality and way of life laid deep in the cultural soil, with the classics etched on the minds of those fortunate in their education. Chang'an was the geographic and heartfelt home of this new Chinese nation, the focus both of its political power and of its intellectual and artistic acumen. These two faces of the city, political and artistic, forged perhaps the greatest fault line of classical Chinese poetry.

Mount Zhongnan was the favourite escape of scholars and civil servants tired of the capital and its trappings, or of those who had lost their position at the court. Lying a little outside the city, it was surrounded by silence and mountains, where a poet could contemplate nature and pursue a more Daoist way of life, shunning the strictured, Confucian ways of the court.

It also afforded a vexed courtier the chance to reflect on how far emperor and court had strayed from the Confucian ideal, or to bemoan the injustice of his own lot, perhaps the victim of jealous courtiers or simply of poor imperial appointments. Some of China's most vivid poetry was written among the bamboo groves of these southern hills.

BAN GU

Rhapsody on the western capital

That then they stopped and went no further, going west and
    building our supreme capital there.

Have you, my host, heard of the ground for this, and have you ever
    surveyed the state and order of Chang'an?'

    . . .

Heaven and man being here in responsive harmony, royal
    intelligence was displayed . . .

avour was extended to the West, here in very truth the capital was
    built.

    . . .

The walls were [as] of iron, a myriad spans in extent; the
    encircling moat dug deep as an abyss.

Three stretches of highway were laid out, twelve gates of ingress
    and egress were erected.

Within were the streets and cross-streets, the ward gates numbered
    a thousand.

Nine market places were opened, the merchandise displayed, kind
    by kind in ordered rows.

[The throng was so great] men could not face about,

the carriages [so many] they could not make a turn.

The town was so full that it overflowed into the suburbs,

With a hundred stores on either side . . .

The red dust rising everywhere, the smoke [of the fires] linking in
    clouds.

Thus numerous and thus rich was the populace, its gaiety without
    limit . . .

Its knights for hire looked like dukes and marquises, its shop girls
    more sumptuous than great ladies.

. . .

[The Imperial palace]

Here were ornate gate-towers reaching up into the sky, here
    crowning the hill were the vermilion-shaded halls.

Built of rare materials, its rafters were shaped like dragons' pinions,
    its pillars had bases constructed of jade, the rich interlacing of
    colours making an impression of luminous splendour.

. . .

In the buildings to the left and right were the locations for the
    hundred officers of state:

Where Xiao, Cao, Wei, Ping, made their policies for the sovereign.

As they lent strength to the mandate of heaven, so they handed
    down the sovereign rule, and as they gave wings to the
    government, so they made civilisation [for the people],
    spreading afar the magnanimity of Great Han, removing the
    poisoned stings of derelict Qin.

. . .

Here also were the Tian Lu and Shi Chu [buildings], where the
    archives were kept, where venerable elders patient in
    instruction, famous Confucians and learned scholars were
    commanded to expound and discuss in relation to the
    Scriptures [or 6 Arts], to scrutinise and collate in relation to the
    disagreements and agreements.

Here also were the Cheng Ming and Chin Ma chambers where the
    work of composition went on, where fine poets and men of
    penetration congregated.

Having gone to the roots of things, and having exhausted seeing
    and satiated hearing, they unfolded sectioned compositions,
    compared and regulated abstruse patterns of diction.

Then the buildings housing court functionaries:

Here were gathered the officers of rites and ceremonies, men who
    had come first in the examinations, the upright and the filial

from a hundred prefectures: officers of the guards, keepers of
the robes, controllers of eunuchs, guardians of the gates,
halberdiers of the throne room – a hundred different offices,
each with its prescribed duties.

  . . .

[the Qian Chang palace outside the walls:]

  . . .

in ascending it, before one is halfway in the ascent of the tower,
    the eyes swing round and the attention is astray.
One loses hold of the railing and thus misses its support, is about
    to fall headlong but yet held back.
In bewilderment of soul from loss of [sense of] distance – round one
    turns in one's tracks and goes down step by step to the bottom.
(So splendid are the imperial gardens)
An abode for immortals – not a place where we mortals can find
    peace.

Ban Gu (32–92 AD) was the court historian in the Eastern or
Later Han dynasty (25–220 AD). He was one of the three
authors of the immortal *Book of Han*, the history of the dynasty
completed in 111 AD. The three authors were all from the Ban
family, including Ban Gu's younger sister. As well as
genealogical tables the history includes dozens of short essays
on subjects from astronomy to literature to law.

    Ban Gu's other most famous work was the poem from which
the verses above are taken. The novella-length poem is narrated
by a Chang'an resident arguing its merits over Luoyang. There
are those, it says, who 'boast of the ancient institutions of the
western city, Chang'an, aiming to disparage the eastern city,
Luoyang. Consequently, I have composed these poems on the
Two Capitals to expose the errors in these men's minds and to
confound them by the beautiful ordinances of the present.'

ZHANG HENG

Rhapsody on the western capital

The Qin line having their base in Yung, where the soil is rich, became strong; Zhou, being in Yu, became weak. The first emperor of Early Han made his capital in the west, and was lavish; the first emperor of Later Han dwelt in the east and was frugal.

The Shen Ming* tower reared itself aloft and the Chang kan tower,
    in a hundred piled-up storeys,
One storey succeeds another, as you go up and up – you catch sight
    of the North Star, and are thrilled with delight.
Rising from the world's dust into the upper air,
You spy out the long back of the curving rainbow: you study the
    leaning together of the Hyades. If you go on to the flying balcony
    and look beyond, you observe straight before you Jade-Light and
    String-of-Jade.
You are about to go on – but before you have gone halfway you are
    shaking with fear, filled with apprehension.
Without the Tu Lu's [climber's] agility, who can climb high and
    keep going higher?

Not all is well, however, as the gluttony of the palace pursuits
    suggest tomorrow may be less well catered for.
Overweening lust for hunting and fishing, exertions capturing small
    fry.
Ransacking and scouring, womb-grabbing and egg-snatching:
Snatching at pleasure today, have I leisure to pity what comes after
    me tomorrow?
In a time of settled peace, how realise it will totter to ruin?

The emperor, later intoxicated by the goings on, heads out of the palace incognito and into a harem.

For many years this was so, two hundred seasons and more: merely
    the soil was fertile, the outlands productive, all commodities in
    heaped abundance: the high passes bringing safety on every
    hand, forming a girdle easy to protect.
Those who had gained them had the power; those in possession of
    them endured in the land.
Where a stream flows it is hard to stop, where the roots are deep
    [the three] can hardly rot.
The result was a dissolute temper of luxury in excess – a sweet
    odour became pungent and more and more rank.

The writer concludes by saying he was born three hundred years after the start of the Han, when the emperors are Lord of all, and the inheritance is greater than ever. But parsimony now rules: 'Is it not true that what we want we cannot get and what we cannot get we want?'

Zhang Heng (78–139 AD) was a scholar and statesman of such diverse interests that he has often been dubbed a 'Renaissance man'. An inventor and a scientist, Zhang Heng created the first seismometer and improved the accuracy of the Chinese calculation of pi. He was also a literary scholar and author and the poem above satirises the western capital by juxtaposing its physical majesty with its dissolute and voracious court. The western and eastern cities referred to at the beginning of this extract are, respectively, Chang'an and Luoyang.

---

* spirit-showing

WANG CAN

Seven sorrows

The western capital in lawless disorder
wolves and tigers poised to prey on it
I'll leave this middle realm, be gone,
go far off to the tribes of Ching.
Parents and kin face me in sorrow,
friends running after, pulling me back.
Out the gate I see
only white bones that strew the broad plain.
A starving woman beside the road
Hugs her child, then lays it in the weeds,
Looks back at the sound of its wailing,
Wipes her tears and goes on alone:
'I don't even know when my own death will come –
How can I keep both of us alive?'
Whip up the horses, leave her behind –
I cannot bear to hear such words!
South I climb the crest of Pa-ling*
turning my head to look back on Chang'an.
I know what he meant – that falling spring† –
sobbing racks my heart and bowels.

---

* Baling (Pa-ling in the translation above) was the site of the tomb of the
  Western Han emperor Wen, whose rule was a peaceful, golden era.

Wang Can (177–217) was both scholar and politician, known for helping to pen laws for the state and for being one of the renowned seven scholars of Jian'an. The above poem is his most famous. Its skilful portrait of a people under siege marks Wang out as both a poet-craftsman and a man overwhelmed by the suffering of his countrymen.

The China Wang inhabited was enduring a period of disarray and uncertainty, leading the poet to depict 'wolves and tigers' preparing to attack the city. In 190 Dong Zhuo had sacked Luoyang, abducted the emperor of the Eastern Han at Luoyang, and carried him to Chang'an. In 192 fighting broke out between Dong Zhuo's generals in Chang'an. Wang Can decided to seek refuge with Liu Biao, governor of Jingzhou (Jingman), who had been a student of his grandfather. He wrote these verses as he fled Chang'an around 195 AD, bound for the wilder regions of the upper Yangzi.

† Falling spring refers to a poem in the *Classic of Poetry* (number 153), China's earliest poetry collection, in which some of the poems are almost three thousand years old. It includes the lines:

> Biting chill, that falling stream
> that soaks the clumps of asphodel
> O how I lie awake and sigh
> thinking of Zhou's capital.

CEN SHEN

Moving with my army on the ninth day I think of my gardens in Chang'an

Most strongly do I wish to scale the heights
No one comes with wine.
Far away, I pity the chrysanthemums of my garden,
Blooming by the battlefield.

The 'double ninth' (day nine of the ninth month) was usually a day for family reunions, and the chrysanthemum would be used for autumn wine – 'jiu' means both nine and wine, and the day was associated with longevity. Linking this day to the battlefield shows how all is awry.

Born in 715, Cen was a recluse at Songyang near Luoyang in the years 729 to 734, and submitted work to the civil service examiners without taking the test, only to be rejected. In 744 Cen received the coveted *jinshi* degree (or civil service certificate), and in 751 fought in the losing army in the battle of Talas, the great encounter between Han China and the impressive warriors of a new faith from the west, Islam. The poet spent much of his career in Chang'an, where he held a number of senior positions, such as head of the governing body of the arsenal, and also of forestry.

Cen wrote the poem following in 758, a few months after Emperor Suzong's triumphant return to Chang'an following its recapture from the An Lushan rebels. The poet Jia Zhi then invited three highly distinguished colleagues, among them Cen Shen, to write their own versions. The four poems that resulted have been subject to comparison by Chinese scholars ever since.

CEN SHEN

The morning audience at Daming Palace, presented to friends and colleagues of the two ministries

Silver candle to the morning audience, the purple road is long,
Spring hues of the Forbidden Quarters, gris-green at dawn.
A thousand wings of frail willows droop before blue scrollworks;
A hundred calls from flitting bush warblers fill Jianzhang Palace.
Sound of swords and pendants attends the jade courtyard
    footsteps;
Attire of caps and robes teased by the royal censers' fragrance.
Together we bathe in the gracious waves of Phoenix Pond;
Morning after morning, moistening my brush, I wait upon my lord.

DU FU

Straddling the sky

Its height straddles the grey sky;
The piercing wind never ceases.
Since I do not have an enlightened man's heart;
Climbing it, perversely, brings a hundred cares.
Only now do I know that the power of teaching by symbols
Is worthy of pursuit in depth.
Overhead we thread through the caverns of dragons and
    serpents;
First we emerge from the gloom of beams and spans.
The seven stars are at the Dipper;
The sound of the Heavenly River flows westwards.
Xi He, the charioteer, whips the white sun;
Shao He moves the clear autumn.
The Qin mountain suddenly shatters;
The waters of the Jing and Wei cannot be found.
How can one discern the royal domain?
Turning my head I call for Shun.
The clouds over his grave are sorrowing.
Alas for the revel at Jasper Pond,
As the sun sets over Mount Kunlun.
The yellow swan leaves and does not stop,
With plaintive cries, where will it go?
Look at the geese following the sun,
Each with its own plan for millet and rice.

The prolific Du Fu (712–770) brushed out at least 1,500 new
poems during his life and ranks as one of the country's greatest

poets. He lived in the great age of poets too, the High Tang, which spanned the second to seventh decades of the eighth century AD. A master of the various forms of Chinese poetry, Du Fu failed to enter the civil service and saw China riven by rebellion from 755. This widespread suffering became a focus of his poetry. But he wrote about urban splendour too.

One of the wonders of Tang Chang'an was the Temple of Compassionate Mercy. Cen Shen (above) inaugurated another round of poetry on the subject of an ascent to the stupa of this temple. Built in 652 and known as the tumulus of the western regions, it lay west of Vermilion Bird Gate, on the site of an old temple from the Sui dynasty (581–618 AD). It had the best bamboo grove in the capital and looked out on to the emperor's canal. Winners of the *jinshi* degree were asked to inscribe their names there.

In Du Fu's submission, the poet subverts the idea of physical elevation being allied with spiritual elevation, an association already at least nine centuries old in China. As the narrator ascends the mountain, he does indeed enter a mythological realm, but his search for space and time is frustrated by mist.

Teaching by symbols is a reference to Buddhism. The Jing waters of line 14 flow from two sources in Gansu province to join the River Wei at Gaoling, and were said to be as clear as the Wei's waters were muddy. The yellow swan is a mythical bird, the vehicle of immortal beings. Qin mountain is another name for Mount Zhongnan, the retreat of scholars and poets outside Chang'an. Xi is charioteer of the sun, Shao Hao the god of autumn. Lines 17 and 18 concern the sage king Shun, buried at Cangwu. The jasper pond is where the queen mother of the west held a banquet in honour of King Mu of Zhou.

Some traditional commentators read the poem as allegorical (common for Du Fu) – the dalliance of Xuanzong with Lady Yang at the hot springs at foot of Mount Li are implied by this reading, Shun representing Taizong, whose devotion in dedicating a stupa to his consort mother contrasts with his descendant's licence with the concubine Yang. The blurred vista of lines 13 to 16 underlines the moral confusion of the day when light and dark (like the rivers Jing and Wei) are no longer distinguishable. The yellow swan stands for men who flee for an uncertain destination, while the wild geese are men who serve the emperor out of self-interest alone.

Such opaque references appear throughout much Chinese poetry, as the poet seeks to criticise the emperor for the sake of the country or of fellow intellectuals, but without ever expressing direct disapproval. Thus a poem about the flight of a bird or the blooming of a flower could be deeply political in its intent.

For many of the best civil servants, poetry provided the only outlet when the court had been overrun by palace eunuchs or brought into moral disorder by a wanton emperor. The frustration of such men, their skills wasted as the kingdom disintegrates, forms one of the fault lines of classical Chinese poetry.

DU FU

This stream of yours

This stream of yours, as though borrowed from the blue Yangzi,
This bit of mountain sliced off from the Jieshi rocks:
Green dangling, bamboo shoots broken in the wind;
Red splitting open, plums fattened by the rain.
A silver pick to strum the many-stringed zither,
A golden fish exchanged for another round of wine.
We'll move as fancy takes us – don't bother to sweep –
Sit wherever we please on the mossy ground.

Du Fu wrote this poem on a trip in 752–3 to the Zhongnan
mountains outside Chang'an, that favourite haunt of exiles,
writers and frustrated civil servants. *Jieshi* is a northern Chinese
rock formation. A 'golden fish' was a decorative girdle worn by
officials, but it has here been sold for wine, testament to its
owner's new priorities.

DU FU

Ballad of the beautiful ladies

Third month, third day, in the air a breath of newness;
By Chang'an riverbanks the beautiful ladies crowd,
Rich in charms, regal in bearing, well-bred, demure,
With clear sleek complexions, bone and flesh well-matched,
In figured gauze robes that shine in the late spring,
Worked with golden peacocks, silver unicorns.
On their heads what do they wear?
Kingfisher glinting from hairpins that dangle by the sidelock borders.
On their backs what do we see?
Pearls that weight the waistband, subtly set off the form
Among them, kin of the lady of cloud curtains, pepper-scented halls

   . . .

Humps of purple camel proferred from blue cauldrons,
Platters of crystal spread with slivers of raw fish;
But ivory chopsticks, sated, dip down no more,
And phoenix knives, in vain hasten to cut and serve.
Yellow Gate horses ride swiftly, leaving the dust unstirred,
Bearing from royal kitchens unending rare delights.
Plaintive notes of flute and drum, fit to move the gods,
Throngs of guests with their lackeys, all of noblest rank

   . . .

a bluebird flies off, in its bill a crimson kerchief.
Where power is all-surpassing, fingers may be burned.
Take care, draw no closer to his Excellency's glare!

This poem, set during the spring outing held on the third day of the third lunar month at Qujuang Park in Chang'an, is an attack on the Yang family, who counted among their number the beautiful Yang Guifei, Emperor Xuanzong's favourite. Thus, 'pepper-scented halls' refers to Yang Guifei's perfumed palace, while the bluebird, mentioned towards the end, was used to carry love messages, and Yang Guifei's cousin, the senior civil servant Yang Guozhong, was rumoured to be having an affair with her, despite social codes governing kinship relations. In the ballad, her sisters appear as the ladies of Guo and Qin.

Yang Guifei is the most famous concubine in Chinese history and known as one of the 'four beauties of ancient China', all remembered for their excessive influence over the emperors who fell in love with them. Yang had lived as a Daoist nun, but the emperor grew besotted with her, granting her all sorts of exceptional privileges, such as bathing in the pool of the emperors at his palace. Historians still debate whether she was more manipulative arriviste or ill-fated scapegoat.

DU FU

Lamenting autumn rains

Blusterous winds, unending rains, autumn of chaos,
The four seas, eight directions one solid cloud:
Horses going, cows coming, who can make out for sure?
Muddy Jing River, clear Wei, how to tell them apart?
From grain tips, ears sprouting, millet heads turned to black;
No word of how farmers, farmers' wives are faring.
In the city, exchange a bed of quilt, get a meagre peck of grain –
Just agree, don't argue over which is worth more!

In this poem, Du conjures the destructive rains of the autumn
in 754. Just as the loss of the Jing and Wei's distinctiveness
illustrated the moral confusion of the time, so the rain and
winds act as a metaphor for the problems faced by Han China
including, presumably, inflation.

DU FU

Plain-garbed man

Plain-garbed man of Chang'an, who takes note of him?
Crude gate closed, he keeps to his country plot.
The father goes nowhere, mugwort and brambles grown rampant,
Though his little ones, no worries, race around in wind and rain.
Rain hiss-hiss, bringing the cold on early;
From the north, wild geese, wings dampened, can barely fly on
    high.
Since the start of autumn, not once have we seen the white sun.
This earth of ours, muddy, foul – when will it ever dry?

Du Fu's failure to qualify for the civil service meant he was
obliged to lead a simple life. Thus we find him living in Duling
suburb with his family, wearing not the robes of state but the
unremarkable clothes of unrecognised men.

DU FU

Pitying the prince

Over Chang'an walls white-headed crows
Fly by night, crying above Greeting Autumn Gate.
Then they turn to homes of the populace, pecking at great
    mansions,
Mansions where high officials scramble to flee the barbarians.
Golden whips broken, royal steeds dropping dead,
Even flesh and blood of the ruler can't get away in time.
How pathetic – costly disc of green coral at his waist,
The young prince standing weeping by the roadside!
I ask, but he won't tell me his name or surname,
Says only that he's tired and in trouble, begs me to make him his
    servant.
A hundred days now, hiding in brambles and thorns,
Not a spot on his body where the flesh is untorn.
Sons and grandsons of the founder all have high-arched noses;
Heirs of the Dragon differ naturally from plain people.
Wild cats and wolves in the city, dragons in the wilds,
Prince, take care of this body worth a thousand in gold!
I dare not talk for long now, here at the crossroads,
But for your sake, prince, I stay a moment longer.
Last night, east winds blew rank with the smell of blood,
From the east came camels crowding the old capital.
[so called because the emperor no longer lived there]
These Shoufang troops, good men all –
Why so keen, so brave in the past, so ineffectual now?
I've heard the Son of Heaven has relinquished his throne,
But in the north his sacred virtue has won the Uighur khan to our
    side.

The Uighurs slash their faces, beg to wipe out our disgrace.
Take care, say nothing of this – others wait in ambush!
I pity you, my prince – take care, do nothing rash!
Auspicious signs over the five imperial graves never for a moment
    cease.

In 756, Du Fu was arrested by rebels who had invaded Chang'an.
Many people were robbed and slaughtered by the new armies
and the poet's 'white-headed crows' augured ill for the capital.
'Greeting Autumn Gate' had been the displaced Emperor
Xuanzong's exit route. The troops had been 'brave in the past'
when they defeated the Tibetans and even now the Uighurs
(who live in northwest China to this day) slash their faces to
show their allegiance to the Chinese ruler. Yet the capital is
overrun.

During the capital's occupation Du Fu remained under effective
house arrest in Dayun Temple until his escape in 757, when he
was able to join the court-in-exile. The last line indicates that
Heaven will not allow the Tang dynasty to pass altogether.

DU FU

Dayun temple, Abbot Zan's room

My mind is in a realm of pure crystal,
Clothes dampening in springtime rain,
I walk slowly through a succession of gateways,
To the inner garden and its sequestered meeting.
Doors open and close just as I reach them,
A bell strikes, hour for the monks' meal.
This ghee gives lasting nourishment to innate nature,
This food and drink support a faltering body.
Many days the Abbot and I have been arm-in-arm companions,
Speaking our mind without timid evasions.
Yellow warblers traverse the rafters,
Purple doves fly down from eave guards.
I've chanced on a spot that suits me exactly,
Strolling among blossoms as slowly as I please.
And to lift my spirits, Tang Xiu here
Smiles, urging me to write a poem.

Tang Xiu was a renowned Buddhist thinker of the fifth century but Du Fu is actually referring to the abbot himself. Like Daoism, Buddhism was often a natural retreat for educated men unable to work or simply for those dismayed by the suffering and chaos around them.

DU FU

Chessboard city

I've heard them say Chang'an's like a chessboard;
Sad beyond bearing, the happenings of these hundred years!
Mansions of peers and princes, all with new owners now;
In civil or martial cap and garb, not the same as before, here.
Over mountain passes, due north, gongs and drums resound;
Wagons and horses pressing west speed the feather-decked
    dispatches.
Fish and dragons sunk in sleep, autumn rivers cold;
Old homeland, these peaceful times, forever in my thoughts.

Du Fu wrote this overview of the city itself after the fall of
Guizhou province. It was included in *Autumn Meditations*, a
collection dominated by regret, as Du Fu laments the political
disorder of the day and his own ailing health and fallen career.
Chang'an becomes a site for warfare, as Du describes military
preparations to block Uighur invasions from the north – the
feathers worn by military messengers won them fast passage.
Du Fu was not the only Chinese poet to liken Chang'an to a
chessboard; Bai Juyi used the same simile.

DU FU

Kunming Lake

Kunming Lake, work project of Han times,
Yet before my very eyes, Emperor Wu's flags and banners!
Weaving girl, loom threads idle in the evening moonlight;
Stone whale, scales and carapace wobbling in the autumn wind.
Waves float wild rice grains, blackening the sunken clouds;
Dew chills the lotus calyx, its spilled pollen red.
From this border outpost to the end of the sky, a road only birds
    can travel.
Here where rivers and lakes strew the earth, one old fisherman.

A little west of the city lay Kunming Lake, engineered under
Han dynasty Emperor Wu. Wu used it for practicing naval war-
fare but here Du Fu uses the Han times as a commentary on his
own era, the Tang. Both the weaver and the whale were statues,
the first on the lake's shore, the second in the lake itself.

LI BAI

Autumn song

Chang'an – one slip of moon
In ten thousand houses, the sound of fulling mallets.
Autumn winds keep on blowing,
All things make me think of Jade Pass!
When will they put down the barbarians
And my good man come home from his far campaign?

The fulling mallets were used to pound out clothes when they were being washed in the river. Chang'an's ten thousand houses are symbolic. Ten thousand has long been one of the most sacrosanct numbers in China. Even when Mao Zedong founded the People's Republic of China in 1949, he stood on top of Beijing's Gate of Heavenly Peace (Tiananmen) before banners which read: The People's Republic of China. May it last ten thousand years!

Li Bai (701–762) remains China's consummate poet. Never able to sit still, he spent most of his life wandering through China, sometimes working for the emperor but usually making a living with his verse. A lover of wine and nature, Li had an extraordinary gift for friendship. His poetry still resonates in translation hundreds of years later, for its ability to speak to the soul through the most spontaneous and simple of lines. It has been said that whereas the best poetry of the Song dynasty (960–1279) was made, the best poetry of the Tang dynasty (618–907) was found. Among the Tang poets, Li Bai's ability to pen verses lacking in artifice but pregnant with power was unrivalled.

The story of his demise captures the romance and spontaneity of his life. Li had been drinking and fell out of his boat into the Yangzi River, trying to embrace the image of the moon dancing on its surface.

LI BAI

A Song of Chang'an

My hair had hardly covered my forehead.
I was picking flowers, paying by my door,
When you, my lover, on a bamboo horse,
Came trotting in circles and throwing green plums.
We lived near together on a lane in Ch'ang-kan,
Both of us young and happy-hearted . . .
At fourteen I became your wife,
So bashful that I dared not smile,
And I lowered my head toward a dark corner
And would not turn to your thousand calls;
But at fifteen I straightened my brows and laughed,
Learning that no dust could ever seal our love,
That even unto death I would await you by my post
And would never lose heart in the tower of silent watching . . .
Then when I was sixteen, you left on a long journey
Through the Gorges of Ch'u-t'ang, of rock and whirling water.
And then came the Fifth-month, more than I could bear,
And I tried to hear the monkeys in your lofty far-off sky.
Your footprints by our door, where I had watched you go,
Were hidden, every one of them, under green moss,
Hidden under moss too deep to sweep away.
And the first autumn wind added fallen leaves.
And now, in the Eighth-month, yellowing butterflies
Hover, two by two, in our west-garden grasses
And, because of all this, my heart is breaking
And I fear for my bright cheeks, lest they fade . . .
Oh, at last, when you return through the three Pa districts,
Send me a message home ahead!
And I will come and meet you and will never mind the distance,
All the way to Chang-feng Sha.

LI BAI

Descending Mount Zhongnan to the kind pillow and bowl of Husi

Down the blue mountain in the evening,
Moonlight was my homeward escort.
Looking back, I saw my path
Lie in levels of deep shadow . . .
I was passing the farm-house of a friend,
When his children called from a gate of thorn
And led me twining through jade bamboos
Where green vines caught and held my clothes.
And I was glad of a chance to rest
And glad of a chance to drink with my friend . . .
We sang to the tune of the wind in the pines;
And we finished our songs as the stars went down,
When, I being drunk and my friend more than happy,
Between us we forgot the world.

Li's influence on Chinese poetry was enormous and his direct students included Du Fu himself. For centuries Chinese scholars and poets have copied out his verses and tried to imitate his style.

But his influence extends to the beginnings of modern western poetry too, when Ezra Pound used his pared down style to forge his own. Ezra Pound was the leading light among the Imagists, described by T. S. Eliot as the founders of modern poetry. Pound and his co-Imagists sought to retrieve a more classical, direct form of poetry, spared the artifice and emotionalism of Longfellow and

Tennyson. When, in 1915, he edited a collection by the poet Lionel Johnson, Pound praised the collection because it had, he said, 'a simplicity like the Chinese.'

As for Pound himself, his greatest Chinese influence was Li Bai, that master of economy and of the spare and striking line. Ezra Pound's *Cathay*, a 1915 translation of Chinese verse, most of it Li Bai's, was the landmark work in Pound's quest to forge a fresh poetry, shorn of historical references and flowery language.

WANG WEI

The Zhongnan mountains

Its massive height near the City of Heaven
Joins a thousand mountains to the corner of the sea.
Clouds, when I look back, close behind me,
Mists, when I enter them, are gone.
A central peak divides the wilds
And weather into many valleys . . .
Needing a place to spend the night,
I call to a wood-cutter over the river.

Wang Wei (699–759) was another of the Tang greats, a poet
with an aristocratic background and one who came first in the
civil service exam nationwide. He is best remembered for his
poetry and his paintings and his favourite subject was always
nature, even if he sometimes viewed it with the wry eye of the
Buddhist who believes it may not be real after all. Mountains,
mist, water and bamboo groves form the landscape of his poetry,
while his vision of the natural world is that of a ranging eye not
interested in picking out details but in capturing the entirety
and unity of what he sees.

WANG WEI

My retreat at Mount Zhongshan

My heart in middle age found the Way.
And I came to dwell at the foot of this mountain.
When the spirit moves, I wander alone
Amid beauty that is all for me . . .
I will walk till the water checks my path,
Then sit and watch the rising clouds –
And some day meet an old wood-cutter
And talk and laugh and never return.

WANG WEI

Looking down in a spring-rain on the course from fairy-mountain palace to the pavilion of increase harmonizing the emperor's poem

Round a turn of the Qin Fortress winds the Wei River,
And Yellow Mountain foot-hills enclose the Court of China;
Past the South Gate willows comes the Car of Many Bells
On the upper Palace-Garden Road-a solid length of blossom;
A Forbidden City roof holds two phoenixes in cloud;
The foliage of spring shelters multitudes from rain;
And now, when the heavens are propitious for action,
Here is our Emperor ready – no wasteful wanderer.

BAI JUYI

Written while on night duty at the palace, to send to Yuan Ninth

Ten thousand threads of thought, two sheets written:
Before sealing them, I read them over, wonder if they'll do.
The palace water clock has just sounded the fifth watch [4am],
The lamp in the window, my one light, about to go out.

Bai Juyi (772–846) was a civil servant who saw both high rank and exile apportioned to him during his long career. Careful to preserve his own works, some 2,800 poems survive. His poems display a lively social conscience as well as a love for thoughtful retreat and Buddhist reflection. His famous friendship with the poet Yuan Chen was carried out in verse too, since the two were usually posted to distant places: 'we two duckweeds adrift on vast oceans,' as Bai once wrote to his old friend.

In Bai's poetry we see a complete adult life written out, perhaps the most intimate depiction surviving of the inner life of one of classical China's great men: as a poet, a bereaved father, a civil servant, a friend, a Buddhist and an exile.

BAI JUYI

A quiet house in Chang-lo ward

The emperor's city, a place of fame and profit:
from cockrow on, no one relaxes.
I alone play the idler
the sun high, my hair as yet uncombed.
The clever and the clumsy differ in nature;
advancers and laggards go separate ways.
Luckily I've happened on a time of great peace
when the Son of Heaven loves scholars and learning.
With small talent it's hard to perform great services:
I collate texts in the Palace archives.
Out of thirty days I spend twenty at the office,
and so get to nurture my perversity and sloth.
A thatched roof, four or five rooms,
one horse, two hired men,
a salary that runs to 16,000 cash –
it gets me through the month with some to spare.
So I'm not pressed for clothing and food,
likewise little bothered with social affairs.
Thus I can follow my youthful inclinations,
passing day after day in constant quietude.
But don't suppose I'm lacking in friends;
the bustler and the quiet one each has his own crowd.
There's seven or eight men of the Orchid Terrace
who do the same sort of work I do.
But on my days off, I'm robbed of their talk and laughter,
morning and night I long to see a caller's carriage.
Who can find time from chores of collating,

loosen his belt and stretch out in my hut?
In front of the window there's bamboo for diversion,
outside the gate, a shop that sells wine.
And what do I have to entertain you?
A few stalks in the background, a pot of brew.

BAI JUYI

Light furs, fat horses

A show of arrogant spirit fills the road;
a glitter of saddles and horses lights up the dust.
I ask who these people are –
trusted servants of the ruler, I'm told.
The vermilion sashes are all high-ranking courtiers;
the purple ribbons are probably generals.
Proudly they repair to the regimental feast,
their galloping horses passing like clouds.
Tankards and wine cups brim with nine kinds of spirits;
from water and land, an array of eight delicacies.
For fruit they break open Tung-ting oranges,
for fish salad, carve up scaly county from Tien-chih.
Stuffed with food, they rest content in heart;
livened by the wine, their mood grows merrier than ever.
This year there's a drought south of the Yangzi.
In Chuchou, people are eating people.

Bai Juyi's disgust at the starvation suffered by the poor while the emperor's court feasts highlights what he saw as his greatest responsibility as a poet: social critique. Anticipating Zola or Dickens, this critical role was also meant to be played by the good Confucian official, even if it meant sacrificing success in his career. Bai paid for it with exile.

BAI JUYI

Climbing the terrace of Kuanyin and looking at the city of Chang'an

Hundreds of houses, thousands of houses – like a great chessboard.
The twelve streets like a huge field planted with rows of cabbage.
In the distance I see faint and small the torches of riders to the
    court,
Like a single row of stars lying to the west of the Five Gates.

BAI JUYI

Passing Tianmen street in Chang'an and seeing a distant view of Zhongnan mountains

The snow has gone from Zhongnan; spring is almost come.
Lovely in the distance its blue colours, against the brown of
the streets
A thousand coaches, ten thousand horsemen pass down the
Nine Roads;
Turns his head and looks at the mountains – not one man!

This is typical of Bai's split loyalties and passions, a man divided
between court and countryside and never fully satisfied in either.

BAI JUYI

Song and dance

In Chang'an the year draws to its close;
A great snow fills the Royal Domain.
And through the storm, on their way back from Court,
In reeds and purples the dukes and barons ride.
They can enjoy the beauty of wind and snow;
To the rich they do not mean hunger and cold.
At a grand entry coaches and riders press;
Candles are lit in the Tower of Dance and Song.
Delighted guests pack knee to knee;
Heated with wine they throw off their double furs.
The host is high with the Board of Punishments;
The chief guest comes from the Ministry of Justice.
It was broad daylight when the drinking and music began;
Midnight has come, and still the feast goes on.
What do they care that at Wenxiang tonight
In the town gaol prisoners are freezing to death?

BAI JUYI

An early levee (addressed to hermit Chen)

At Chang'an – a foot full of snow;
A levee at dawn – to bestow congratulations on the Emperor
Just as I was nearing the Gate of the Silver Terrace,
After I had left the ward of Hsin-chang
On the high causeway my horse's foot slipped;
In the middle of the journey my lantern suddenly went out.
Ten leagues riding, always facing to the north;
The cold wind almost blew off my ears.
I waited for the bell outside the five gates;
I waited for the summons within the Triple Hall.
My hair and beard were frozen and covered with icicles;
My coat and robe – chilly like water.
Suddenly I thought of Hsien-yu valley
And secretly envied Chen Chu-shih,
In warm bed socks dozing beneath the rugs
And not getting up till the sun has mounted the sky.

BAI JUYI

The ill-fortuned house

Chang'an has many great mansions,
they crowd the avenues east and west.
But sometimes within their red-lacquered gates
Rooms and galleries stand empty.
Owls hoot from pine and cassia branches,
Foxes hide in thickets of orchid and crysanthemum;
Somber mosses, yellow leaves strew the ground,
And at twilight the scudding winds keep whirling by.
The first owner was a general and statesman,
Accused of misconduct, exiled to the Pa-yung border.
His successor, a high-ranking court official,
Took sick and died in these rooms.
Then four or five tenants in succession
Met one unhappy event after another
Wind and rain have made holes in the eaves,
Snakes and rats burrow through the walls.
People, suspicious, no longer dare to buy;
Day by day the builders' work tumbles into decay.
Ah, that the minds of unenlightened people
Should be so stupid and obtuse!
They only fear disaster will overtake them,
Never stop to think where it will come from.

Bai is keen to overturn popular superstitions in this poem. His lesson remains unstated but his own encounters with professional disaster may have left him with a keener sense of the transience of success and stability – where others might blame their street address for their fall from grace.

BAI JUYI

Library in autumn

Pagoda tree flowers bright with rain, new autumn in the land;
Paulownias leaves wind-tossed, sky verging on evening;
All day in the back office, nothing to do,
The senior librarian, white-haired, sleeps with his head on a book.

BAI JUYI

FROM *Liaoling**

. . .
Who does the weaving, who wears the robe?
A poor woman in the glens of Yueh, a lady in the palace of Han.
. . .
For dancing girls of Chaoyang, token of profoundest favour,
one set of spring robes worth a thousand in gold –
to be stained in sweat, rouge-soiled, never worn again,
dragged on the ground, trampled in mud – who is there to care?
The Liaoling weave takes time and toil,
Not to be compared to common *tseng* or *po*;
Thin threads endlessly plied, till the weaver's fingers ache;
Click-clack the loom cries a thousand times but less than a
    foot is done.
You singers and dancers of the Chaoyang palace,
could you see her weaving, you'd pity her too!

* A kind of fine silk.

BAI JUYI

FROM *Pouring out my feelings after parting from Yuen Chen*

Drip, drip the rain on paulownia leaves;
softly sighing, the wind in the mallow flowers.
Sad, sad the early autumn thoughts
that come to me in my dark solitude.
How much more so when I part from an old friend –
no delight then in my musing.
Don't say I didn't see you off –
in heart I went as far as the Green Gate and beyond.
With friends, it's not how many you have
but only whether they share your heart or not.
One who shares my heart has gone away
and I learn how empty Chang'an can be.

LI BAI

Drinking alone by moonlight

Here among flowers one flask of wine,
with no close friends, I pour it alone.

I lift cup to bright moon, beg its company,
then facing my shadow, we become three.

The moon has never known how to drink;
my shadow does nothing but follow me.

But with moon and shadow as companions the while,
this joy I find must catch spring while it's here.

I sing, and the moon just lingers on;
I dance, and my shadow flails wildly.

When still sober we share friendship and pleasure,
then, utterly drunk, each goes his own way –

Let us join to roam beyond human cares
and plan to meet far in the river of stars.

Li Bai wrote this poem shortly before leaving the city. As ever,
the moon was his muse, whether sober or drunk.

LUOYANG

There has been a city called Luoyang on the central Chinese plain for four thousand years and it is meant to sit at the heart of the whole country. A key moment for the city was when it became the capital of the Eastern Zhou dynasty in 771 BC, effectively making it senior among the capitals of China's various kingdoms, since the Zhou dynasty were the royal *primus inter pares* of the various regional ruling families.

The various kingdoms were united to form China in 221 BC but Luoyang was not capital of a unified China until 25 AD, when it became capital of the Eastern Han. The flowering of a productive artistic culture ensued but this efflorescence was cut short in the mid-second century as civil war enveloped the country. The city was burnt down in 189 when, according to one of the Chinese chroniclers, 'within the city walls the devastation was total.'

Rebuilt in the year 200, Luoyang reached a new cultural climax in 265 but was then dragged into wars from 291–306 and sacked in 311. In 336 it was briefly the southern capital for a northern kingdom and another brief period of use ended in 399. Han rule was restored (from the south) in 416, until the barbarian Northern Wei dynasty took the city in 423, expanding the population to half a million in thirty years, but the Song forced the Wei to abandon it in 430.

In 493 a new emperor chose it as his Chinese capital, and 493–502 saw a building project to create a complete Han city; non-Han languages were even banned at court. By 502 there were palaces and government offices, and the walls were almost done. Next came private residences. From 515 Empress Dowager Hu ruled for five years. The state became rich in grain in 516 and there was peace. Dowager Hu built monasteries and nunneries. The 400-foot high Yung-Ming pagoda was the most spectacular, with a ninety-foot mast at the top. Many magnificent temples were raised inside and outside the city. But in 528, seven thousand Erhchu invaders entered Luoyang and massacred around two thousand people. Briefly resurrected in 532, the city was abandoned in 534.

In scale, Luoyang rivalled classical Rome, medieval Constantinople and Chang'an. In the sixth century it already had 109,000 households according to the poet Yang Xuanzhi but more recent estimates quote closer to 600,000, as well as good roads and water channels which irrigated imperial gardens and ran into lakes. Moreover, it had been created from nothing.

The palace dominated both topographically and emblematically. Yang praised the city for its strong literary culture but clearly considered it middlebrow. Buddhist literature was exceptionally important – the religion was popular with rich and poor alike and was twined with Chinese folk religion. Chan, Madhyamika and Pure Land Buddhism all thrived and there was an insatiable demand for new Buddhist thinking, spawning a diplomatic and religious expedition to Gandhara in 518, which brought back 170 sutras and sastras. Daoism was overshadowed.

Around 605, the Sui emperor Yang Di sent two million labourers to rebuild Luoyang a few miles west of the Northern Wei ruins – this is today's city. According to Ban Gu's pro-Luoyang narrator-poet, the emperor 'crossed the Great River and strode over North Peak, he named his regime and established his capital at Luoyang.' This followed, the poem says, a period of wanton death, after which the people cried out and heaven gave its mandate to Guang Wu. What followed was a period of restoration of the traditions of the ancient king Yao. The people were fed, human relations appropriately ordered. In imperial China the four crucial relationships were reckoned to be between husband and wife, man and man, father and son and between emperor and subject, thus mimicking the approach of the ancient sage Fu Xi. The new emperor first toured his empire, seeing what each region had in plenty and where it lacked, before extending the city of Luoyang, 'fanning it out on a grand scale, in towering grandeur and resplendent symmetry; embellishing the Han capital in the midst of Chu Xia [China], making a control for all parts of the world and forming their crowning point. Here within the city royal houses were resplendent, revealing a divine artistry, which prodigality could not surpass, which frugality could not call prodigal.'

From here, says the writer, the royal influence heads in all four directions, even beyond the borders of his own land, as far as Yunnan to the distant south. Moreover the emperor, afraid that extravagance might be the country's ruin, encouraged frugality and moderation, and emphasised not the arts but farming and the planting of mulberry trees. As fine silks become viewed as a disgrace, so the people were cleansed from decadence and learned contentment.

Luoyang had geographical advantages too. It was militarily better situated than Chang'an (which was remote from the Yangzi valley). It had mountains to the south, east and west, and was close to the Yellow River. It also had symbolic importance, as the Luo, Yi and Qian rivers were the old centre of Chinese civilisation. In Luoyang, it was said, 'ten thousand places converge like the spokes of a wheel.'

Yang Xuanzhi, a court official of the period, wrote a good deal about the city. Those same forces that deserted Luoyang in 534 AD seemed to oppose Han culture in general. Yang wished to remember not just the old capital but the loss of imperial legitimacy, as the state orders the killing of leading gentlemen and their families. He is especially critical of the Erhchu from Shanxi who killed the court and the aristocracy in 528, and sacked the city in 530. Fu Yi (554–639) described Yang (in *Kao shih chuan*) as one of eleven 'men of high understanding' who opposed Buddhism. But Yang was also recording lost splendour – he seems to regret the destruction of Buddhist buildings. Yang was a court guest from 528–30, a prefect of Chicheng, second assistant to a general, third grade keeper of the palace archives (with access to state documents), and a Wei loyalist. Yang was translator of Chinese Buddhist texts into Chinese language and wrote the *Stories about Buddhist Temples in Luoyang*.

Luoyang thrived once more under the Tang dynasty. First it was made capital in 657 due to the periodic famines striking Chang'an. Then, in 691, the empress Wu, who favoured the city, moved more than half a million people there from Chang'an and its environs. The city was now home to a million.

ANON

Cypresses green

Cypress on grave mound, green so green,
and in the ravine, rocks heaped in piles.
Man is born between earth and sky;
he goes swift as a wayfarer travelling far.
So take your joy in beakers of ale,
pour it full, not stingily;
Drive the cart harder, lash on the nag,
in Luoyang and Wan good times are had.
Luoyang is a city teeming full,
where fine hats and sashes seek out their own.
Narrow lanes through the thoroughfares
with many great houses of princes and earls.
Two palaces face each other afar,
paired towers, a hundred feet high and more.
So feast to the end, give the heart glee,
why let grim woes beset you?

Although there are poems that probably date to around 1,000 BC, the classical corpus is usually dated either from the seventh century BC or from the beginning of the Han dynasty, which began late in the third century BC and saw the introduction of the five-syllabic form, which heralded an escape from the grand and impersonal subjects of the more ponderous, older form.

This later stage was identified by Stephen Owen, the poem's translator, as the true beginning of the classical tradition. It was a tradition which would span two millennia. The *Nineteen Old Poems*, from which the verses above are taken, appeared during its infancy, in the second century AD. Like its early peers, the collection made no mention of its author.

Some poems in the collection focus on the pain of parting, but feasting was another theme common within the early classical output. In the poem above, which draws on old Chinese folk songs, it is doubtless the anarchy of late-second-century China that makes the poet so keen to enjoy immediate pleasures while he can, before the 'grave mound' claims him.

ANON

Nineteen old poems

XIII

I drove my wagon out Upper East Gate
And gazed at far tombs north of the walls.
Winds whistled in silver poplars
Cypress and pine lined the wide lanes.
Beneath them lay men long dead,
Fading into the far endless night.
They sleep under Yellow Springs sunken from sight,
And never will wake in a thousand years.
Shadow and light move in endless floods,
Our destined years are like morning dew.
Man's life is brief as a sojourner,
Old age lacks the firmness of metal or stone.
They have brought men here for thousands of years,
A span unmatched by good man or Sage.
With pills and diets men seek the Undying,
And are usually duped by elixirs.
The better way is to drink fine ale
And dress yourself in satin and silk.

The eastern gate exit was clearly a memorable route since it is mentioned in a number of poems. But here the stillness of the great city, its cypresses and pine, lead the poet not to glory in its power but to reflect on the transience of human life. While some seek immortality with elixirs, a widespread obsession in ancient China, others find pleasure in alcohol and comfort in fine clothes.

CAO ZHI

The ruins of Luoyang

I climb to the ridge of Peimang hills
And look down on the city of Luoyang.
In Luoyang how still it is!
Palaces and houses all burnt to ashes.
Walls and fences all broken and gaping,
Thorns and brambles shooting up to the sky.
I do not see the former old men;
I see only the new young men.
I turn aside, for the straight road is lost;
The fields are overgrown and will never be ploughed again.
I have been away such a long time
That I do not know which path is which.
How sad and ugly the empty moors are!
A thousand miles without the smoke of a chimney.
I think of our life together all those years;
My heart is tied with sorrow and I cannot speak.

Cao Zhi (192–232) was an important general but his priority
was clearly stability rather than militaristic adventures. While
many poems had opened with a departure from the city's east
gate towards the hills, Cao here upturns the order, as the
narrator surveys the deserted city from the hills. The narrator
can only lament Luoyang's destruction and its subsequent
blanketing by thorns and thistles.

CAO ZHI

How desolate is Luoyang

How desolate is Luoyang,
Its palaces burned down,
The walls fallen in ruins,
As brambles climb to the sky . . .
There are no paths to walk,
Unworked fields have run to waste . . .
Lonely is the countryside,
A thousand *li* without one smoking hearth

A *li* is around half a kilometre. Thus, Cao's poem sees destruction not just in the city but throughout the countryside too. The fields around Luoyang are some of the oldest farmland in the world, but here they lie empty and unworked.

There is a deeper context to Cao's ruminations on disorder and suffering too. His own father Cao Cao was the warlord who controlled the north of the country, while his brother Cao Pi became the older man's successor. This left Cao Zhi out of power and in danger from his own kin. When Cao Zhi felt the yoke of his brother's restrictions on him, he turned to poetry to vent his frustration. He was the greatest poet of his era.

MENG HAORAN

Song of a girl from Luoyang

There's a girl from Luoyang in the door across the street,
She looks fifteen, she may be a little older . . .
While her master rides his rapid horse with jade bit and bridle,
Her handmaid brings her cod-fish in a golden plate.
On her painted pavilions, facing red towers,
Cornices are pink and green with peach-bloom and with
    willow,
Canopies of silk awn her seven-scented chair,
And rare fans shade her, home to her nine-flowered curtains.
Her lord, with rank and wealth and in the bud of life,
Exceeds in munificence the richest men of old.
He favours this girl of lowly birth, he has her taught to dance;
And he gives away his coral-trees to almost anyone.
The wind of dawn just stirs when his nine soft lights go out,
Those nine soft lights like petals in a flying chain of flowers.
Between dances she has barely time for singing over the songs;
No sooner is she dressed again than incense burns before her.
Those she knows in town are only the rich and the lavish,
And day and night she is visiting the hosts of the gayest
    mansions . . .
Who notices the girl from Yue with a face of white jade,
Humble, poor, alone, by the river, washing silk?

Meng Haoran (689–74) arrived in Chang'an as a young man but never succeeded in making a success of a political career, as he had hoped. His dreamy, independent voice helped him to write poetry that was much admired by his contemporaries. Meng's technique here, to slowly build a fabulous picture of wealth and luxury before undermining it with a single, brief comparison or question, was a common approach among Chinese classical poets whose social conscience forged their subject matter.

YANG XUANZHI

Record of the monasteries of Luoyang

With power gone my road of life is short,
Yet in distress the path to death seems long,
Full of regrets I left Luoyang behind;
Sadly I enter now the land of ghosts.
After I am shut inside the tomb,
No more will that dark court see light.
A bird sings pensively among green pines;
Amid white poplars mourns the wind.
Long have I heard it said that death is bitter:
I never thought to bring it on myself.

As mentioned earlier, Yang was a Buddhist translator under the
'barbarian' northern Wei dynasty in the sixth century. He wrote
accounts of the spread of Buddhism into China hundreds of
years earlier. This last poem was sometimes sung by pallbearers
at funerals.

ZHANG HENG (78–139 AD)

Fu on the eastern capital

In this poem, Zhang argued that the Two Passes near Chang'an did not protect the Qin dynasty, but that Luoyang enjoyed 'a wide circumference'.

The poem reads:

> . . .
> with a measuring tablet marked the shadows, neither too short
>   nor too long.
> There at the meeting point of the winds, and rains, he
>   thereafter built a royal city.
> There with the Yellow River at the back and facing the Luo
>   River . . . with the hill slopes and the valleys encircling it.
>
> The wise man, with mystic penetration, discerned the capital,
>   this Luoyang.
> He said 'Abide here'; he said 'Glory will be continuous here'.

New palaces were impressive, too, as the poem relates:

> We pass to Emperor Ming's time . . .
> Then was opened the special gate Southern-Beginning, and the
>   stately structure of the Door-of-Fulfilment.
> Kindness and mercy shone on Honour-for-the-Worthy
>   [another gate], the repute of justice was extolled [in the
>   gate] Winter-Metal.
> Cloud dragons were painted on the gate that led to Eastern
>   Road; Spirit-tigers were depicted in the western quarter.
> The twin watchtowers Symbol of Majesty were built, emblems
>   of the time-honoured standards in the Six Scriptures.

Within the enclosure came Virtue-Embodied, Tower-of-Beauty,
    [the halls], Celestial-Prosperity, Light-Dispensing,
Reviving-Decrees, Welcome-of-Spring, Enduring-Peace,
    Lasting-Repose.Flying galleries through shich the Emperor
    passed like a spirit, unseen by mortal men.

The poet related that, when a hundred dignitaries entered the
room,

The Son of Heaven with three grades of formal bows makes
    ceremonial acknowledgement.
How stately, how majestic!
How correct, how impressive!
Truly the most impressive spectacle in the world!

Formal festivals are celebrated and the first furrow is ploughed
by the emperor. The focus is on the harmony brought about
under the rule of the emperor, in heaven and in the empire. The
Chang'an system was too extravagant, but appropriate frugality
marks the Luoyang emperors, with Confucian self-denial and
Daoist sufficiency guiding.

LI BAI

Spring night in Luoyang – hearing a flute

In what house, the jade flute that sends these dark notes
    drifting,
scattering on the spring wind that fills Luoyang?
Tonight if we should hear the willow-breaking song,
who could help but long for the gardens of home?

Although Li Bai was the journeyman and high priest of the
natural world, at home in the wildness of Sichuan province in
the south, yet he also had ambitions to be a courtier and to rise
in political life. These were never realised and the man himself
was clearly caught between the two lives: one in the great
metropolis and the other in the freedom and comfort of home
in the south. The 'willow-breaking song' was usually sung at
parting, when friends would break off willow wands as parting
gifts.

CAO ZHI

Rhyme-prose on the goddess of the Luo River

. . .

Gaze far off from a distance:
she sparkles like the sun rising from the morning mists;
press closer to examine:
She flames like the lotus flower topping the green wave.
She strikes a balance between plump and frail;
the tall and the short of her are justly proportioned,
with shoulders shaped as if by carving,
waist narrow as though bound with white cords;
at her slim throat and curving neck
the pale flesh lies open to view,
no scented ointments overlaying it,
no coat of leaden powder applied.
Cloud-bank coiffure rising steeply,
long eyebrows delicately arched,
red lips that shed their light abroad,
white teeth gleaming within,
bright eyes skilled at glances,
a dimple to round off the base of the cheek –
her rare form wonderfully enchanting,
her manner quiet, her pose demure.

A tributary of the Yellow River, the Luo River runs through
Luoyang as well as several other ancient Chinese cities. Cao Zhi
penned this poem to the goddess of the river Luo in memory of
a former lover who had passed away. Notice how Cao depicts
her as between plump and frail and between tall and short, a
reflection of the classical Chinese view of female beauty as
being founded in balance.

RUAN JI

Singing of thoughts/Chanting my thoughts

Beautiful trees make paths beneath themselves:
peach and plum in the eastern garden.
Autumn winds toss the drifting bean leaves;
now all things begin to wither and fall.
Brightest blossoms have their fading,
the high hall is grown over with brier and thorn.
Leave it – spur the horses and go,
climb the foot of Western Hill.
Hard enough to keep one body whole;
harder when you long for wife and child.
Chill frost will clothe the grassy meadow,
the year will darken and then be gone.

This poem is thought to describe the poet's visit to Luoyang in 223 to pay his respects to Cao Pi, emperor of the Wei dynasty. Some critics give the poem an allegorical interpretation, suggesting it is a declaration of loyalty to his brother, the emperor.

Ruan was one of the 'seven sages of the bamboo forest', a famous group of writers from the Wei and Jin dynasties, and had a reputation as a Daoist wild man and a drunk – his poetry often focuses on the more mystical questions associated with Daoism.

This is from a series of poems which act as a polemic against the unruliness of the times and the decline of the Cao family rule, the family to which he was loyal. Never explicitly political, Ruan's poems nevertheless had a political subtext. References to autumn, winter and separation may well be political too.

BAI JUYI

The grand houses at Luoyang

By woods and water, whose houses are these
With high gates and wide-stretching lands?.
From their blue gables gilded fishes hang,
By their red pillars carven coursers run.
Their Spring arbours, warmed with caged mist;
Their autumn yards with locked moonlight cold.
To the stem of the pine tree, amber beads cling;
The bamboo branches ooze ruby drops.
Of lake and terrace who may the masters be?
High officers, councillors of state.
All their lives they have never come to see,
But know their houses only from the bailiff's map!

As so often with Bai, the punch is delivered only in the last couple of lines. It is best to depart Luoyang with Bai too, as he makes his final journey to one of its eastern suburbs, Chao village.

BAI JUYI

Chao village

Each year in Chao village pink apricots bloom –
Fifteen years now, how many times have I seen them?
But at seventy-three it's hard to count on another visit.
I've come this spring to say good-bye to the blossoms.

ACKNOWLEDGEMENTS

We gratefully acknowledge permission to reprint copyright material as follows:

The Arthur Waley Estate for permission to use the translations made by Arthur Waley of 'Climbing the terrace of Kuanyin and looking at the city of Chang'an', 'Passing Tianmen street in Chang'an and seeing a distant view of Zhongnan mountains', 'Song and Dance', 'An Early Leveé', 'The Grand Houses at Luoyang', all by Bai Juyi, and 'The Ruins of Luoyang' by Cao Zhi (they all appeared in *Chinese Poems* published by Allen & Unwin in 1946); the assistant editor of *Renditions* who kindly forwarded our letter of request to Professor Burton Watson in Kyoto; Random House Inc. for permission to include the following translations by Witter Bynner from the Vintage (1972) title *The Jade Mountain*: 'A Song of Chang'an', 'Descending Mount Zhongnan to the kind pillow and bowl of Husi' by Li Bai, 'The Zhongnan Mountains', ' My retreat at Mount Zhongnan' and 'Looking Down in a Spring-rain on the Course from Fairy-mountain Palace to the Pavilion of Increase Harmonizing the Emperor's Poem' all by Wang Wei, and 'Song of a girl from Luoyang' by Meng Haoran; OUP USA for permission to include 'How desolate is Luoyang' by Cao Zhi from W. J. F. Jenner's *Memories of Loyang*; W. W. Norton & Company, for permission to use extracts from 'Nineteen Old Poems III', 'Nineteen Old Poems IV' and 'Drinking Alone by Midnight' from *An Anthology of Chinese Literature: Beginnings to 1911*, edited and translated by Stephen Owen © 1996 Stephen Owen and The Council for Cultural planning and Development of the Executive Yuan of the Republic of China; the University of Hawaii Press for permission to use Douglas Dunn's translation of 'I spur my horse past ruins' by Han Shan, from *Popular Songs and Ballads of Han China* (1993), edited by Anne Birrell; Princeton University Press for permission to publish extracts from 'Rhapsody on the Western Capital' by Ban Gu, 'Rhapsody of the Western Capital' by Zhang Heng and 'Rhapsody on the Eastern Capital' by Zhang Heng all from *Wen Xuan or Selections of Refined Literature* (vol. 1), edited by Xiao Tong and David Knechtges (1982) and for permission to use an extract from Yang Xuanzhi's *A Record of Buddhist Monasteries in Luoyang*, translated by Yi-t'ung Wang.

Every effort has been made to trace or contact copyright holders. The publishers would be pleased to rectify any omissions brought to their notice at the earliest opportunity.

A NOTE ON TRANSLATORS

The lives of translators usually pass by unsung. But special mention should be made of the two translators most featured in this collection. Producing translations from Chinese into English that are both accurate and elegant is an enviable achievement in itself, but the unlikely lives of some of the greatest twentieth century Sinologists deserve a look too.

ARTHUR WALEY

Arthur Waley was born Arthur David Schloss in 1889, the son of a Jewish economist, but chose to use his paternal grand-mother's maiden name instead. Waley studied classics at King's College, Cambridge. His career path was set when he was appointed Keeper of Oriental Prints at the British Museum in 1913. Waley had to catalogue the holdings, and taught himself Chinese and Japanese while working at the museum.

In 1918 he met Beryl de Zoete, a dance critic and writer, with whom he lived in Bloomsbury her until her death in 1962. In 1929 he quit the museum to devote more time to his literary interests.

By this time, Waley was already involved with the Bloomsbury Group, the gathering of writers and thinkers who met in Bloomsbury, London through the interwar period to discuss literature, philosophy, feminism, economics, sexuality and aesthetics. Among them were Virginia Woolf, John Maynard Keynes and Lytton Strachey.

Waley's interest in China and Japan brought him into close contact with Ezra Pound, who helped him to organise publication of his first translations.

Waley had works published from 1918 up until the 1960s and they ranged from Buddhist scriptures to Chinese poetry to the fourteenth-century *Secret History of the Mongols*. He translated Loazi's *Dao De Jing* as well as Confucius' *Analects*. In bringing Asian authors to an English-speaking audience, Waley's impact is unparalleled. Yet he never set foot in Asia.

He died in 1966 and was buried in Highgate Cemetery.

BURTON WATSON

Watson was born in 1925 in New Rochelle, New York. At the age of seventeen he dropped out of school to join the navy and ended up working on repair vessels in the South Pacific during the War. In 1945 he made visits to Japan each week while his ship was stationed at Yokosuka Harbour. When he returned to the US after the war, he chose to study Chinese and Japanese at Columbia University and wrote his doctoral thesis on Sima Qian, China's Herodotus. He worked in Japan and the US in the years that followed, translating Buddhist texts and some of the greatest Chinese poets. In 1973 he moved to Japan permanently, where his prodigious output has continued.

INDEX OF POETS

INDEX OF POEM TITLES

INDEX OF FIRST LINES

My mind is in a realm of pure crystal 32
Over Chang'an walls white-headed crows 30
Pagoda tree flowers bright with rain, new autumn in the land
    51
Plain-garbed man of Chang'an, who takes note of him? 29
Round a turn of the Qin Fortress winds the Wei River 41
Silver candle to the morning audience, the purple road is long
    21
Ten thousand threads of thought, two sheets written 42
That then they stopped and went no further, going west and
    building our supreme capital there 13
The emperor's city, a place of fame and profit 43
The Shen Ming tower reared itself aloft and the Chang kan
    tower, in a hundred piled-up storeys 16
The snow has gone from Zhongnan; spring is almost come 47
The western capital in lawless disorder 18
There's a girl from Luoyang in the door across the street 64
Third month, third day, in the air a breath of newness 26
This stream of yours, as though borrowed from the blue
    Yangzi 25
Who does the weaving, who wears the robe? 52
. . . with a measuring tablet marked the shadows, neither too
    short nor too long 67
With power gone my road of life is short 66